Tell Me About
HAJJ™

SANIYASNAIN KHAN

BRACKNELL FOREST
BOROUGH COUNCIL

Goodword
FOR KIDS

First published 2000
Reprinted 2002
© Goodword Books, 2002

Goodword Books Pvt. Ltd.
1, Nizamuddin West Market
New Delhi 110 013, India
Tel. (9111) 435 6666, 435 5454, 435 1128
Fax (9111) 435 7333, 435 7980
e-mail: info@goodwordbooks.com
www.goodwordbooks.com
www.goodwordforkids.com

Photographic Credits:
Peter Sanders, cover (top right, centre,
bottom right), 1, 3 (bottom),
4, 6, 7, 8, 10, 13, 19, 20 (bottom),
23, 25, 27, 29, 31, 33
back cover (middle left);
Mohamed Amin, cover (top left),
spine, 14, 17, 20 (top), 32 (top, middle,
bottom right, bottom);
Aramco World, back cover (top right);
Madan Mehta, cover (bottom left),
back cover (middle right).

Thanks are due to Anna Khanna and
Susan Brady Maitra for their immense
help in making this book possible.

Illustrations: K.M. Ravindran

C O

NTENTS

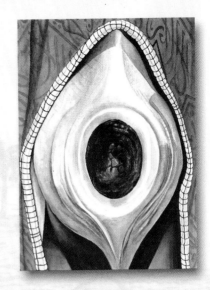

1. God's Best Friend

Long ago, about 4000 years ago, in a faraway place called Ur in Iraq, a child was born whose name was Ibrahim or Abraham. He was so gracious, tender-hearted and pure in faith that Allah gave him wisdom when he was still a child. Allah was so pleased with him that he made him His best friend.

When Ibrahim ﷺ grew up, he became a great prophet, and preached the truth and Allah's message in his country. Later he travelled to Syria, Palestine and Egypt.

When a beautiful son was born to his wife Hagar, Ibrahim ﷺ was ordered by Allah to travel towards what we now know as Makkah along with his wife and the little child, whose name was Ismail or Ishmael. They all travelled for a long time till they reached a lonely, barren valley, near two small hills called Safa and Marwa.

Ibrahim ﷺ asked his wife to stay near one of the hills along with the little Ismail, and started to go away. His wife

How Ibrahim ﷺ Came to Know Allah

When Ibrahim ﷺ was born, the people worshipped stones and statues. Even when Ibrahim ﷺ was still a child he wondered why. When he asked his father, Azar, it only angered him. One day, when Azar and the other townspeople were away, Ibrahim ﷺ took an axe and broke all the idols in the public temple except the biggest. When the people discovered this, they asked Ibrahim ﷺ, "Who has done this?"

"Ask the biggest idol," Ibrahim replied calmly. "Why do you worship things which cannot even talk, move or understand?" The people were speechless, but the urge to do what they found their fathers doing was so strongly implanted in them that they could not understand Ibrahim's message. They became furious, and tried to kill him.

Ibrahim's desire to find the truth grew. One night, while observing the sky, Ibrahim ﷺ noticed a particularly bright star. "This is my Lord," he said. But when it set, he said: "I do not love that which fades." After the same experience with the moon and the sun, Ibrahim ﷺ announced: "I will turn my face to Him who has created the heavens and the earth, and live a righteous life; I am no idolater." (*Surah al-An'am, 6:75-79*).

protested, "Why are you leaving us alone here? Are you leaving us here to die?" But Ibrahim عليه السلام replied, "My Lord has commanded me to do this." Then Hagar, breathing a sigh of relief, said: "If Allah has ordered you to do so, then He will not let us die."

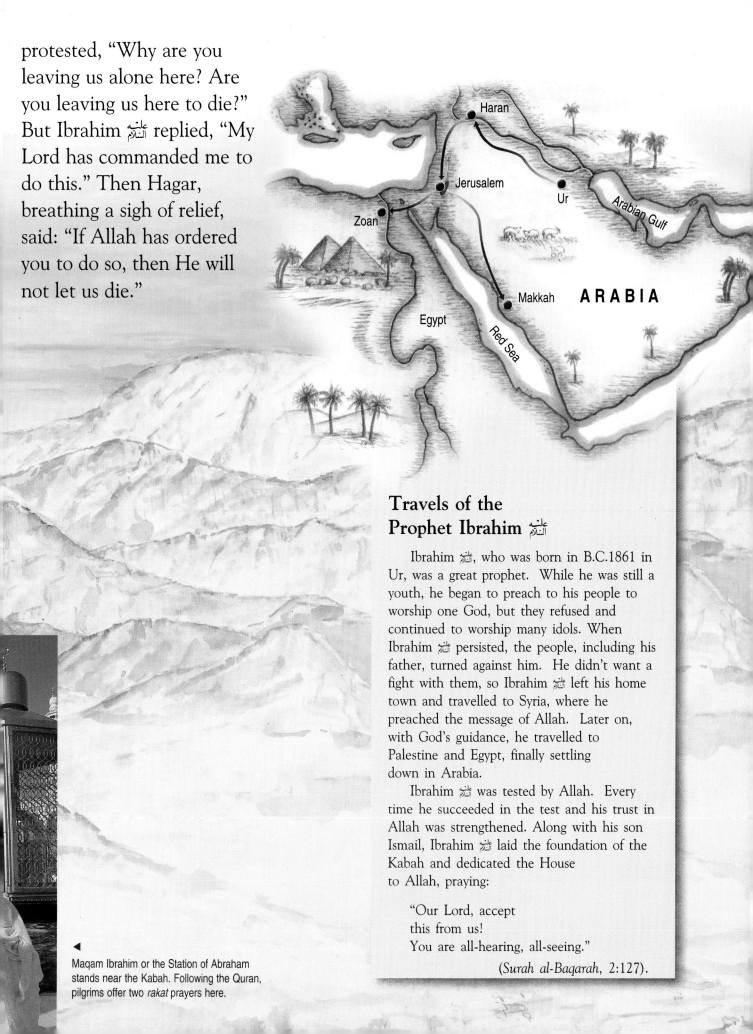

Haran

Jerusalem

Ur

Arabian Gulf

Zoan

Makkah

ARABIA

Egypt

Red Sea

Travels of the Prophet Ibrahim عليه السلام

Ibrahim عليه السلام, who was born in B.C.1861 in Ur, was a great prophet. While he was still a youth, he began to preach to his people to worship one God, but they refused and continued to worship many idols. When Ibrahim عليه السلام persisted, the people, including his father, turned against him. He didn't want a fight with them, so Ibrahim عليه السلام left his home town and travelled to Syria, where he preached the message of Allah. Later on, with God's guidance, he travelled to Palestine and Egypt, finally settling down in Arabia.

Ibrahim عليه السلام was tested by Allah. Every time he succeeded in the test and his trust in Allah was strengthened. Along with his son Ismail, Ibrahim عليه السلام laid the foundation of the Kabah and dedicated the House to Allah, praying:

"Our Lord, accept this from us! You are all-hearing, all-seeing."

(*Surah al-Baqarah*, 2:127).

◄ Maqam Ibrahim or the Station of Abraham stands near the Kabah. Following the Quran, pilgrims offer two *rakat* prayers here.

2. The Miracle of Zamzam

After a while, baby Ismail began to cry for water. But there was not a single drop of water to drink. Hagar ran helplessly from one hill to another, but there was no water, nor any human being to give her water.

As the baby was crying desperately with thirst and the mother was running from one mountain to another, Allah caused a miracle—a spring gushed forth beneath the feet of Ismail. When Hagar saw this from a distance, she shouted, "Zamzam" the sound made by rushing water in the Babylonian language.

Hagar came running and gave some fresh spring water to the thirsty child to drink. And so his life was

Signs of Allah

The two small hills, Safa and Marwa, symbolize patience and perserverance. One of the pilgrim's most important activities is the *sa'y* — walking swiftly between them seven times. *Sa'y* means to struggle, or to do strenuous exercise.

It makes us remember the struggle of Hagar in the desert, rushing anxiously from hill to hill, trying to catch sight of a caravan that would have water for her dying child, and how suddenly from one hill she saw a spring gush forth near her child's feet. Allah had provided for her and her son.

Today the two hills are fully enclosed within the Sacred Mosque, and pilgrims make the seven rounds down mosaic tiled corridors. As shown in the picture, the ailing and disabled are wheeled in chairs down an aisle between the corridors.

◄ The walkway between the two hills, Safa and Marwa.

saved. This spring later on became famous as Zamzam.

Ismail and his mother began to live in the valley and, because of the Zamzam spring, more people gradually came to settle there, slowly building up a small town, which was later called Makkah.

From time to time Ibrahim عليه السلام would visit Makkah to meet his family, especially to see his young

Ismail growing up in the beautiful surroundings of nature—in a new town in a lovely valley surrounded by hills, away from the crowded cities whose inhabitants at that time were mostly idol-worshippers.

Access to the Zamzam area. ▶

The Sacred Zamzam

Zamzam is the name of the well in the courtyard of the Great Mosque in Makkah. Pilgrims to Makkah drink the water of Zamzam which has a special sacredness; some believe it has healing properties. The Zamzan water is a symbol for the basic truth, that when all seems lost, Allah is still present, with healing and life for the soul. After the exertion of the *tawaf* and *sa'y* most pilgrims drink Zamzam and relax at the nearby Zamzam area. Pilgrims drink Zamzam throughout their stay in Makkah and often take home small flasks and jerry cans as souvenirs for friends and relatives who are unable to make the Hajj themselves. Today, Zamzam water is pumped out in channels and provided through taps fitted in the Zamzam area, which is accessible in underground galleries reached by a flight of steps near the Kabah. Men and women have separate entrances.

3. A Special Dream

One night, Ibrahim ﷺ dreamt that he was sacrificing his son, Ismail ﷺ. This was an order from his Lord. Ismail was still a child, but Ibrahim ﷺ told him about his dream. Ismail was a brave boy. He was ready to obey the command of Allah, who had created him. So, without hesitating, he said to his father, "Do what you are commanded, father. God willing, you will find me one of the steadfast."

Ibrahim ﷺ took his son away to sacrifice him. As he reached a place, which is now known as Mina—a

► The valley of Mina, where the incident of the Sacrifice occurred. During the Hajj, pilgrims gather here to complete the rites of stoning.

valley near Makkah—Satan appeared and tried to dissuade him. Ibrahim عليه السلام picked up a few small stones and threw them at Satan. Little Ismail and his mother did likewise.

As Ibrahim عليه السلام took a knife to sacrifice Ismail, Allah sent the angel Jibril (Gabriel) with a ram. "Sacrifice this ram. Do not sacrifice Ismail," said Jibril to Ibrahim عليه السلام.

Allah was so pleased with the readiness of Ibrahim عليه السلام to sacrifice his beloved son, that He commanded the believers to observe this day as Id al-Adha, or the Feast of Sacrifice. Every year Muslims sacrifice an animal in remembrance of Ibrahim's trust in Allah.

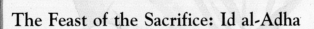

The Feast of the Sacrifice: Id al-Adha

The great act of the Prophet Ibrahim عليه السلام is remembered by all Muslims every year on the 10th Dhul Hijjah, the day which concludes the main rites of the Hajj. Those on the Hajj perform the same animal sacrifice as Ibrahim did. For Muslims all around the world, this is done after the Id prayer.

It is usually performed by the head of a household, who states the proper ritual intention (niyyah) and the names of the person or persons on whose behalf the sacrifice is being made. As it is being done, the words: "Bismillah, Allahu Akbar" are uttered.

The meat is roughly divided into three parts, one for the poor, one for relatives, neighbours and friends, and one for the family who sacrifice the animal. In some countries there are organizations which perform this service on behalf of individuals and the meat is dried up and distributed to the poor.

The Feast of Sacrifice reminds believers of the readiness of the Prophet Ibrahim عليه السلام to give up his most beloved son. Likewise, on this day believers reaffirm their belief in Allah and pledge themselves to parting with their precious belongings, if there is a need for it. The Quran describes these sentiments in the following verse: "Truly, my prayers, my sacrifice, my life and my death all belong to Allah, the Lord of the worlds." (Surah al-An'am, 6:162).

4. Building the Kabah

Ismail ﷻ grew up a strong and loving youth. Ibrahim ﷻ and Ismail ﷻ were ordered by Allah to build the House of God—the Kabah in Makkah. They took stones from the nearby hills and started to work.

The Sacred House

Following the words of the Quran: "Turn your faces towards the Holy Mosque, wherever you be, turn your faces towards it" (al-Baqarah 2:144), over a quarter of the world's population from around the globe orient themselves towards the Kabah in prayer. It was the first shrine built for the worship of the One God.

Neither the Kabah nor the Black Stone are objects of worship: they are symbols (shaairullah) providing a focal point for the unity of all Muslims. The Quran also calls it al-Bayt al-Atiq (the Ancient House), al-Bayt al-Haram and al-Bayt al-Muharram (both meaning the Sacred House).

For this sacred land, Ibrahim ﷻ prayed, "My Lord, make this land secure, and provide its people with fruits, such of them as believe in Allah and the Last Day."

As Ibrahim ﷻ and Ismail ﷻ laid the foundation, they prayed, "Our Lord, accept this from us! You are the

◀ It is towards the Kabah that, five times every day, more than a quarter of the world's population turn themselves in prayer.

All-hearing, the All-seeing." They further prayed, "Our Lord, make us submissive to You, and make our offspring a nation submissive to You and show us our ways of worship." They also prayed for a prophet to be born in their family, who would teach wisdom to the people and purify their faith. Their prayer was answered many years later, when the Prophet Muhammad ﷺ was born to their descendants.

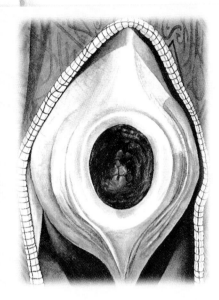

The Black Stone

At the eastern corner of the Kabah, about 5 feet above the ground, there is an oval black stone of about 18 cm in diameter fixed in the wall. It is enclosed in a silver frame and is known as *al-Hajar al-Aswad*, or the Black Stone. This stone was originally set there by the Prophet Ibrahim ﷺ, and is the only relic of the original building.

For this historical reason, the Prophet Muhammad ﷺ showed a great fondness for this stone by kissing it. It is the only thing the Prophet Muhammad ﷺ kept intact when he removed all the idols and reclaimed the Kabah for Allah in 630 A.D.

Following the tradition of the Prophet, the pilgrims of today also kiss and touch it, or if it is too difficult to get near it, just gesture with their hand while going around the Kabah in Hajj and umrah.

Once the Caliph Umar stood in front of the stone and addressed it in these words: "I know quite well that you are nothing but a stone which can do neither good nor evil. Had I not seen the Prophet Muhammad ﷺ kissing you, I would have never kissed you."

5. The First Call to Hajj

Ibrahim عليه السلام was ordered by Allah to clean the Kabah for those who came there to pray, and to call people to Hajj: "Call all people to make the Pilgrimage. They shall come to you on foot and on the backs of swift camels; they shall come from every deep ravine."

Architecture of the Kabah

Made of grey stone taken from the surrounding hills of Mecca, the Kabah is a rectangular building, forty feet in length and thirty five feet in width. Its wall are about fifty feet high and it is raised on a one foot high marble base called *shadharwan.* Its corners are known as *arkan.* The eastern corner is called *al-rukn al-aswad,* after the Black Stone, fixed on this corner. The other three corners are named after the countries they face. The southern corner, facing Yemen, is called *al-rukn al-Yamani;* the northern corner, facing Iraq, is called *al-rukn al-Iraqi;* and the western corner, facing Syria, is called *al-rukn al-Shaami.* Inside the Kabah there are some wooden pillars which support the roof. The walls and the floor are covered with marble.

A thick semi-circular wall of white marble about three feet high runs from the north to the west corner of the Kabah without being connected to it. This is known as *al-Hatim.* At some time in the past this semi-circular space was a part of the Kabah, hence it enjoys a very special status. People pray two *rakah* inside it, as if they were praying inside the Kabah. *Tawaf* is performed from the outside of this wall and, while the *imam* leads the prayer, it is not permissible to pray inside it.

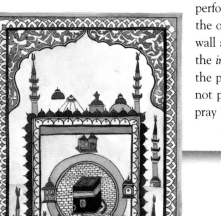

And so Allah made it obligatory for every Muslim male and female to go for Hajj once in a lifetime, provided their means and health permitted. Hajj is one of the five pillars of Islam.

Since then believers from every part of the world go to perform Hajj from the 8th to the 13th of the Islamic month of Dhul-Hijjah. They go to fulfill the command of their Lord and to remember the great act of the Prophet Ibrahim عليه السلام.

Door of the Kabah

The door of the Kabah is on the northern side, some seven feet above the ground level. It is usually covered with a curtain similar to the *kiswa*, but called the *burqa* (the veil). It also bears passages from the Quran. When the door is opened for cleaning, etc, a staircase (*midraj*) on wheels is fixed up to the door.

6. The Prophet Muhammad's Hajj

Ten years after his migration from Makkah to Madinah, the Prophet Muhammad ﷺ performed his Hajj, which came to be known as the "Hajj of Farewell." The Prophet told his followers: "Learn how to perform Hajj, as after this year I may not perform it."

As the news spread around, people from Madinah and nearby areas started assembling there to accompany the Prophet.

On the afternoon of Thursday, 24 Dhul Qada, 10 AH, the Prophet mounted his she-camel and set out for Makkah. A huge crowd of people, over 100,000 in number, accompanied him. Jabir, a Companion of the Prophet, said, "I could see people as far as my eyes could see." On the way more people joined the caravan.

When the Prophet reached a place called Dhul Halifa, he spent the night there and in the morning took a bath and put on *ihram*, the pilgrims' dress made up of two unstitched sheets. (Women wear normal dress and cover their heads with a scarf).

Afterwards he moved towards Makkah saying the *talbiyah* prayer: "Here I am, O Allah! Here I am, at Your service! You have no partner, here I am. All praise, grace and dominion belongs to You. You have no partner." The multitude joined him in repeating these words.

Hajj Caravans

Prior to the age of motor vehicles and airplanes, Hajj pilgrims mainly travelled in caravans by camel. It was a long and difficult journey involving incredible adventure. Pilgrim caravans from Egypt took almost two months crossing the Sinai Desert, risking attack by bandits. Other caravans assembled in Damascus, and those travelers journeyed for as long as thirty days to Makkah.

These huge caravans were like vast, moving cities, some 6000 pilgrims travelling in one group under the command of an *amir al-hajj*, the leader of the pilgrimage, who was like a ship's captain. The pilgrims had to brave certain dangers which would have terrified people even less dutiful to Allah than they were. They had to cross every kind of land, from desert to jungle, and often took years to arrive. One man, single when he left his far-off homeland, arrived in Makkah with a wife and several children. Another man who started out in his youth was in his seventies when he arrived in Makkah. The caravans were accompanied by a troop of soldiers and included outriders, guides, a saddler, a chef, some cooks and a physician or two. In order to avoid the heat of the day, the caravan marched at night. But during winter, they would also travel during the day.

There were several main caravan routes to Makkah. Pilgrims from Turkey assembled in Istanbul and slowly marched across the Anatolian Plateau, gathering pilgrims from every town through which they passed. In Damascus they joined the pilgrims from Syria, then continued across northern Arabia and finally turned south to Madinah and Makkah.

Pilgrims from Iraq assembled in Baghdad and followed the Road of Zubaydah, which went through Najd directly to Madinah and connected with the main road to Makkah. A third route, used by pilgrims from Egypt, ran along the Red Sea coast of Arabia. The pilgrims coming by all these routes converged on Makkah, where they joined other pilgrims who had travelled overland across Africa or sailed west from the Indian subcontinent and the East Indies.

(Adapted from *Aramco and Its World*)

Hajj Pilgrims arriving at Jeddah airport. Modern transportation has greatly eased the pilgrimage, which used to be such a difficult journey for people in the past.

7. Here I Am, O Allah! Here I Am!

After travelling for nine days, the Prophet reached Makkah on 4 Dhul Hijjah. He first went to the Sacred Mosque. On seeing the Kabah, he said: "O Allah! increase the greatness and sublimity of Your House." And further added, "O Allah, You are peace, with You is peace. Our Lord, keep us alive with peace."

Afterwards he performed *tawaf*—going round the Kabah seven times. This is to show how our lives should revolve around our Lord. As he did this, he kept calling upon God: "Our Lord, give us goodness in this world and goodness in the Hereafter, and keep us safe from the fire of Hell."

When he had finished going round the Kabah, he prayed two *rakat* at the Maqam Ibrahim—the Station of Abraham, and went towards the Black Stone

Talbiyah–The Pilgrim's Prayer

Labbayk Allahuma labbayk.
Labbayk la sharika laka labbayk.
Inn al-hamda wan ni'mata laka,
wal mulk, la sharika lak.

Here I am, O Allah! Here I am! Here I am.
You have no partner, here I am.
Surely Yours is all praise, all goodness and
all sovereignty and You have no partner.

This prayer is said over and over again by the pilgrims as they enter Makkah and throughout the Hajj. It is the pilgrim's answer to Allah's call to Hajj. Some recite it with great joy, others are overcome with emotion and weep. To stand in the midst of hundreds and thousands of people and feel that *you* are important to Allah, that He has seen *you* arrive, is an awesome experience that makes you feel humble and happy, sometimes so happy that you cry!

and kissed it. Then he moved towards Safa, saying that Safa and Marwa were signs of Allah. He went up the Safa hill, till he could see the Kabah. The Prophet walked briskly between the two hills seven times and ended the walk at Marwa. Some of the seven laps he did on camel-back. Perhaps he did this so that people could see him from a distance.

The Prophet was staying in Makkah at a place called al-Bath. After staying there for four days, he moved to Mina on 8 Dhul Hijjah and the next morning, he moved off towards Arafat.

Kiswa, the cover for the Kabah

The *kiswa*, made of a mixed cotton and silk brocade, has the *shahada* woven into it: *La ilaha illal Lah, Muhammadur Rasullullah* (There is no deity save Allah, Muhammad is His Messenger). A little above its centre, it is circled by a golden band (*hizam*) covered with passages from the Quran in fine Kufic calligraphy. The inscription there is from *Surah* 3 of the Quran: "The first House founded for mankind was that at Bakka (Makkah), a blessed site, a beacon for the nations" (*Al Imran*, 3:96). The other passages on the *Kiswa* are taken from *Surah al-Kahaf, Maryam, Al Imran, al-Tawbah, Ta Ha, Ya Sin* and *al-Mulk*. The same family has woven the black cloth and embroidered the gold lettering and symbols on the *Kiswa* for generations. The huge cloth measures 232 square yards and weighs 2 tons. The *Kiswa* is changed each year, before Hajj, and the old cloth is cut into pieces for souvenirs for the pilgrims.

8. Arafat Is Hajj

At Arafat, the Prophet stayed in a small tent in the Arnah valley. In the afternoon he rode his she-camel as far as the middle part of the Arafat valley. Here he gave a sermon which is known as the Sermon of the Farewell Hajj. Today, at this very spot there stands a mosque by the name of Nimra.

In his message to humanity, the Prophet emphasised the highest moral values. Here the Prophet announced: "No Arab is superior to a non-Arab and no non-Arab is superior to an Arab. No black man is superior to a red man and no red man is superior to a black, except through *taqwa* or fear of Allah. The most noble among you is the one who is deeply conscious of God."

While the Prophet was praying here, the very last verse of the Quran was revealed to him, and so the Holy Book was completed.

After delivering the sermon, the Prophet performed two prayers together—*Zuhr* and *Asr*.

The Prophet's Farewell Message

At the top of the two-hundred-feet-high Mount of Mercy, the Prophet Muhammad ﷺ, seated on a camel, preached his last sermon to a crowd of over 100,000 in 632 A.D. Here are some of the things the Prophet Muhammad ﷺ told his followers:

- All believers are brothers.
- You must live in peace with one another.
- Everyone must respect the rights and properties of his neighbours.
- The practice of usury is banned—that is the lending of money in such a way that the borrower is forced to pay back much more than he took.
- There must be no rivalry or enmity among you.
- You are to look after your families with all your heart.
- I am leaving behind me two things—the Quran and the example of my life: if you follow these, you will not stray from the right path.
- Worship God, be steadfast in prayer, fast during Ramadan, and pay alms to the less fortunate.

Then the Prophet came to the spot in Arafat which is known as the "standing place." Here the Prophet prayed till sunset. He said that the prayer of this day was the best of all.

The Prophet was praying with divine feelings. The people around him were also praying, some standing, some mounted on their animals—weeping and crying to their Lord for His favours, vowing repentance and craving His blessing.

It was such a great moment that the Prophet said, "Arafat is Hajj."

He prayed, "O Allah, You are listening to me. You are watching my place. You are aware of my hidden and open affairs. I am miserable and needy, I am pleading to You. Asking Your protection..."

The Standing of Arafat

The high point of the Hajj is the "standing" or mass assembly on the slopes of Mount Arafat and in the plains of the valley on the 9th day of Dhul-Hijja. Having left Mina at sunrise, the pilgrims stand in the blistering heat at Arafat from noon until sunset. When the sun crosses the meridian and travels beyond its zenith, pilgrims combine midday and afternoon prayers one after another. They stand in humility and prayer, concentrating only on God. The most heartfelt prayers are offered for the forgiveness of one's sins as well as the welfare of others. Everyone calls upon God in his own way: standing or sitting, motionless or walking about, or even mounted.

The "standing" at Arafat symbolizes the Day of Resurrection, when everyone will stand before God to be judged. At sunset, a sermon is delivered from the top of Mount Arafat. Then the pilgrims proceed to Muzdalifah.

The Mountain of Mercy in Arafat, where the Prophet Muhammad delivered his Farewell Sermon in 632 A.D.

9. On the Way to Mina

After sunset, the Prophet rode towards Muzdalifa. He asked Usama ibn Zayd to ride his camel too. He went on saying *Labbayk Allahumma Labbayk*—"Here I am, O Lord. Here I am." And the people were chanting the same. The Prophet asked people not to run, but to move slowly and calmly, as running was not an act of reverence.

On reaching Muzdalifa, the Prophet asked his Companion Bilal to give the call for prayers. There he said the *Maghrib* and the *Isha* prayers

Resting at Muzdalifa

This open plain lies roughly half-way between Arafat and Mina. Here, until midnight, the massive crowd of pilgrims pray and rest, and each gathers tiny stones for the visit to Mina.

The ancient town of Mina is where Ibrahim was tempted by Satan, as he was on his way to carry out Allah's order to sacrifice his son, Ismail. Satan tried to persuade Ibrahim to disobey God's command, but Ibrahim would not be swayed. There are three stone pillars (*jamarat*) in Mina representing the devil, and pilgrims celebrate Ibrahim's great faith by throwing seven stones at each of them.

◀ An aerial view of the pilgrims' tents at Mina.

together. The Prophet took rest at night and in the morning, after praying, he went towards a place called Mashar Haram where he again prayed.

Before sunrise, the Prophet left Muzdalifah for Mina, after picking up small pebbles.

On the way, passing through the valley of Muhssar, he asked people to move fast, as this was the place where the People of the Elephant, who had come to destroy the Kabah, were punished by Allah. This incident happened in the year in which the Prophet was born, and surah 105 of the Quran describes it.

The code of conduct for Hajj

Besides the prescribed simple clothing, there is a set of specific rules to strengthen *ihram*. They are:

- No fighting or quarreling.
- No telling of lies.
- No swearing or profanity.
- No false accusations.
- No slandering or back-biting.

These five "don'ts" also apply to everyday life, but they are even more important during Hajj.

The code of conduct alsmo includes the following prohibitions:

- The killing of animals or insects, except for fleas, bedbugs, snakes and scorpions. The eggs of birds may, however, be broken or cooked. This is to curb aggression and feel unity with God's creatures
- The hunting of game or inciting others to do so. This is to develop mercy.
- The cutting or pulling out roots of plants, trees, grass and other kinds of vegetation. This is to encourage a love of nature.
- The covering of the head. But people may use umbrellas to protect themselves from the sun. This is to express humility.
- The use of jewellery, perfume, scented soap or body oil. This is to show simplicity.
- The cutting or shaving of hair or the clipping of finger nails. This is to show non-interference with nature.
- The wearing of full shoes. Pilgrims should not wear socks or such shoes as cover the middle part of the foot. There they should use slippers or sandals.
- Flirtatious thoughts of the opposite sex. No one may get engaged to be married during Hajj. Even if husband and wife are both on Hajj, they are not allowed to cohabit.

10. The Stoning Pillars

Riding on, he reached the Jamarat, the three pillars at Mina. He cast seven pebbles at each, saying "Allahu Akbar" each time. The Prophet gave his second sermon at Mina. As in the sermon at Arafat, the Prophet Muhammad ﷺ told the pilgrims to respect and care for each other, and follow God's word in the Quran.

Afterwards the Prophet offered his sacrifices, shaved his head and took off the ihram—the pilgrims' dress. That was the day of the feast—(today we remember that day as Id al-Adha).

On the same day, the Prophet rode to Makkah, performed *tawaf*, drank water at Zamzam and returned to Mina. At Mina people came to him, asking many questions about the pilgrimage. Some said, "I delayed in doing so and so," or "I performed something before it was due," and so on. Over and over the Prophet told them: "No objection, no objection! Objections are only for the

Ihram — More Than a Form of Dress!

Ihram is the name for the particular clothing pilgrims wear. But from the Prophet Muhammad's time *ihram* has meant more than that; wearing it is a sign of the special way pilgrims live while they are on Hajj.

Each pilgrim gets rid of his selfishness, and the petty jealousies and concerns of ordinary life, and dedicates himself to prayer and worship of Allah. He feels truly sorry for his sins, and seeks God's forgiveness. He lives as simply as possible, and promises in his heart to trust in Allah and become good and pure and loving toward others.

First, normal clothing is put away. Male pilgrims wear just two sheets of unsewn white cloth, one wrapped round the waist and the other over the left shoulder. Women pilgrims wear a plain, ankle-length, long-sleeved garment, and a veil covering the head. They must uncover their faces, as a sign of confidence in the atmosphere of purity and goodness of the pilgrimage.

In *ihram* the men and women of all countries, all races and all stations in life look alike. No one can then take pride of place over another. After all, in the eyes of Allah, all men are equal. Just think how He has created us all from a single set of parents—Adam ﷺ and Hawwa (Eve).

Whether a person is rich or poor, black or white, handsome or plain, fast or slow, famous or unknown, clever or ordinary, has successes or failures—is not important. What matters is the sincerity of his striving for goodness and his faith in Allah.

That is *ihram*, the reverent state of mind that is specially heightened during Hajj. Each pilgrim strives for this attitude within himself. He purposely ignores the many frustrations and irritations and inconveniences he may encounter in the crowds at Hajj, and concentrates on God.

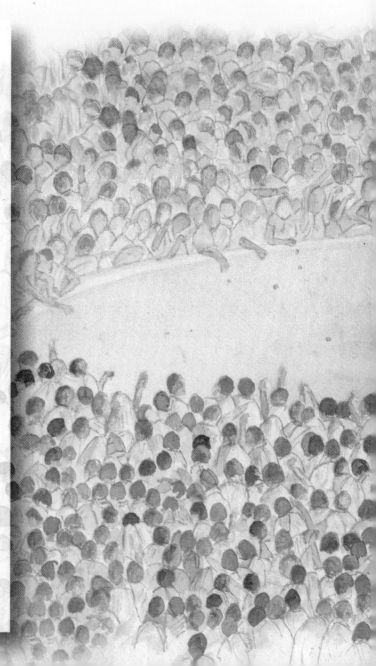

person who wrongfully violates the honour of his fellow-man."

At Mina the Prophet spent three more days for the throwing of stones. In the afternoon of the third day, the Prophet moved to Makkah, where he stayed in a tent and slept briefly. Before the morning prayer, he went to the Sacred Mosque and performed the *tawaf* of Farewell.

The Prophet stayed in Makkah during Hajj for 10 days. Afterwards he left for Madinah. At a place called Dhul Halifa he rested for the night, and at sunrise entered his beloved city— Madinah, the Radiant.

When he first saw the city dwellings from a distance, words of praise poured from his lips: "Allah is most High. There is no deity save Him. He is One. No one is His partner. He is Lord of everything. All praise belongs to Him and He empowers all things. We are returning repentant, praying, prostrating ourselves, praising our Lord. Allah has kept His promise."

The Prophet died two months after performing his Hajj.

Close-up of the Jamrah or the stoning pillar, where pilgrims are carrying out the rites of stoning.
▼

11. Making the Hajj Today

Today, in answer to the original call of the Prophet Ibrahim ﷺ, and following the footsteps of our beloved Prophet Muhammad ﷺ, over two million people from every corner of the globe gather at Makkah to perform their Hajj every year.

When the pilgrim performs the Hajj, he is filled with awe, for he feels he is leaving his own world and entering that of God. He feels so close to God, standing there at Arafat on the very spot where the Prophet delivered his last message to humanity.

Now he is touching the Lord, revolving around Him, running towards Him, journeying on His behalf, making sacrifices in His name, throwing pebbles at His enemies, praying to the Almighty and having his prayers answered. Indeed, to go on Hajj is to meet

A Purposeful Life

When the Prophet Ibrahim ﷺ carried out his divine mission 4000 years ago, he set an example of correct and purposeful living for all those who came after him throughout the ages. The different aspects of such a life are shown by the ritual of Hajj. The stages Ibrahim had to go through are symbolically observed by the pilgrims.

Going on Hajj, therefore, is practising to lead a purposeful life, such as Ibrahim did. The decision to follow his lead is shown by the pilgrims' wearing *ihram* to perform the prescribed rituals.

A life with worthwhile goals will be a very active one, like the Prophet Ibrahim's, and will need a focus. Pilgrims show their realisation of both these points by walking around the Kabah. They also run between Safa and Marwa to show that they are willing to play their part.

People with this sense of purpose willingly sacrifice whatever it takes to attain their goal. During Hajj, they sacrifice an animal. They also join hands with others in the common cause to strengthen their movement. Pilgrims gathered on the plains of Arafat show the same strong feeling of unity.

Hajj is not the end. It is just the beginning. The Prophet Ibrahim ﷺ wanted to reform people by bringing them the message of Islam. Performing Hajj is, in fact, a way of behaving which shows the firm resolve to keep the tradition of Ibrahim alive. The true pilgrim is one who returns from Hajj full of this resolve and all the proper feelings which go along with it, to spread the message of Islam effectively in word and deed.

one's Creator. The pilgrims complete Hajj with that same feeling of awe, but also with a great sense of peace. And if they now have that sense of peace, it is because, having shed their sins on the Plain of Arafat, they have been relieved of their burdens in Islam. In them has been born the spirit of caring for others and a sense of wonder at all the marvellous things Allah has given them.

The Supreme Act of Worship

The Prophet Muhammad ﷺ calls Hajj, the journey to God, the "supreme act of worship." It is a way for Muslims to renew their religious enthusiasm and their faith in Allah. After this, the greatest act of the pilgrims' life, they become like new human beings.

In spirit, it combines all the other acts of worship, helping us to remember Allah and make sacrifices for His sake. On this we have to expend time, money and energy. But Hajj is not just going to and from Makkah. Hajj shows how close we can get to Allah in this life. While other acts of worship are about remembering God, Hajj is about reaching Him. Generally, when we worship God, we cannot see Him, but during Hajj, we come face to face with Him. When pilgrims stand before the House of God, it is like standing before God Himself. Then they are moved to walk around God's House, like a butterfly circling a flower.

The plain of Arafat, where the pilgrims spend one day, is like a picture of Judgement Day. The Quran says, "When the trumpet is blown, behold, from the graves they rush forth to their Lord." (*Surah Ya Sin*, 36:51). And indeed, thousands and thousands of God's servants flock in from all sides to witness the event. And what a great sight it is! All are dressed in the same, simple attire and all recite the same words: "Here we are at Your service, Lord."

Just as the Sacred Mosque in Makkah is the holiest, so is the worship that is performed there—as part of the pilgrimage—the most important. It is not just the pilgrims' duties during Hajj that make it important, but the spirit in which they carry them out.

Pilgrims performing *tawaf* of the Kabah with a feeling that they will revolve forever around ▼ their Lord, putting their entire trust in Him.

12. The Sacred Mosque of Makkah

The Sacred Mosque of Makkah has been made larger over the years. Now the spring of Zamzam and the Safa and Marwa hills are enclosed within its walls, and there is enough space for one million pilgrims at a time. During Hajj this magnificent structure itself seems to float on the ocean of pilgrims that surrounds it as far as the eye can see.

As the pilgrims of different races, speaking different languages, return to their homes, they carry with them wonderful memories of the great men of the past—the Prophet Ibrahim ﷺ, the Prophet Muhammad ﷺ, his Companions and their wives, the great Caliphs, the respected scholars and thinkers of Islam—all who have undertaken the Hajj before them. They will always remember that great coming together, where rich and poor, black and white, young and old, met as equals. They go back, their faces shining with hope and joy, for they have carried out God's command—the same command that He gave to mankind many centuries ago to go on the pilgrimage. This was so that people could not only seek pardon for their sins, but could also turn into better human beings. When they return, it is with the prayer that God may be pleased with their Hajj.

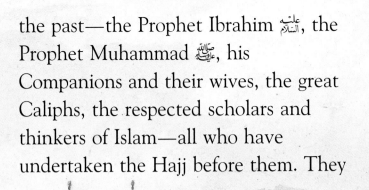

The Sacred Mosque now encompasses fully 356,000 square meters (88 acres), including the rooftop prayer areas and the open plazas surrounding the mosque. Although it comfortably holds a million worshipers, during Hajj and Ramadan more than twice as many pack into it and fill its adjoining plazas.

13. A Visit to Madinah

Madinah, where the Prophet Muhammad's mosque and grave are situated, also attracts pilgrims in great numbers.

On September 20, 622 A.D., the Prophet and his Companions arrived here from Makkah. This journey, which is called *hijrah*, marked the beginning of the Muslim calender. When the Prophet arrived at Madinah, two orphans, Sahl and Suhayl, offered to gift him a piece of land on which to build his mosque. Unwilling to accept the land as a gift, the Prophet paid 10 dinars for it. A temporary mosque made from trunks of palm trees was built, in the construction of which the Prophet himself took part. Since then the mosque has been made bigger and bigger. Within the mosque was the Prophet's own house where, to strengthen their faith, people used to gather to listen to the Quran and the Prophet's wisdom. It was here that a major portion of the Quran was revealed, memorized and written down.

Though this is not part of Hajj, the pilgrims, because of their great reverence for the Prophet, stay there for a few more days to pray in the Prophet's mosque and visit places of historical interest.

The Prophet's Mosque and its surrounding plazas can hold over a million worshippers at a time. Over the years the mosque has been expanded over an area roughly as large as that of the entire city which used to inhabited during the Prophet's life time.

14. The Message of Hajj

One special aspect of Hajj is that it makes people remember Allah's scheme of things, first made known in the Prophet Ibrahim's day, and fulfilled in the days of the Prophet Muhammad ﷺ.

The rites of pilgrimage represent different stages of this scheme. Just as Ibrahim عليه السلام left his native land, Iraq, for Hijaz, the pilgrims leave their homes and depart for the Holy Land. Nearing Makkah, they exchange their tailored clothes for two unstitched sheets like the simple cloths worn by the Prophets Ibrahim and Ismail. When they reach Makkah, they walk around the House of God, just as the Prophet Ibrahim and Ismail had done to solemnise their covenant with Allah.

Standing before the Kabah is as if standing before God Himself. Thus pilgrims are moved to walk around the Kabah, like a butterfly circling a flower.

▼

Then the pilgrims perform *sa'y*, which means walking seven times between the hills of Safa and Marwa in memory of the Prophet Ibrahim's wife Hagar's search for water. At Mina, Ibrahim عليه السلام, ready to sacrifice his son at God's command, was allowed by God to sacrifice a ram instead. In memory of this, the pilgrims do likewise. Then, just as Ibrahim عليه السلام had thrown stones at Satan, who tried to thwart God's will, they throw stones at three pillars, the Jamarat. All throughout, the pilgrims keep saying, "Here I am at Your service, Lord."

The assembly of all the pilgrims on the plain of Arafat is spiritually the high point of the pilgrimage. Here they all promise Allah to model their lives on the example set by the Prophet Ibrahim, Hagar and Ismail, doing God's bidding, whatever it may be, basing their lives on truth and, if necessary, giving up life's comforts and pleasures. God will be their focus, a goal from which they will never be diverted by the forces of evil.

The Spirit of Hajj

All acts and sites of Hajj convey a spiritual message. Pilgrims perform Hajj not just to have their sins pardoned, but to become good human beings, learning to care for others and to wonder at Allah's marvellous gifts.

The Kabah attracts more people than any other building in the world. Over a quarter of the world's population say their prayers facing towards it five times a day. Day and night, year after year, worship never stops there even for a second. It reminds us of life's goal: to worship our Lord, revolve around Him, be close to Him, ask His blessing and put our entire trust in Him. The Prophet was told to tell God's servants that He was near them and answered their prayers. "Therefore, let them answer My call and put their trust in Me, so that they may be rightly guided." (*Surah al-Baqrah*, 2:186).

Tawaf, or going around the Kabah, means revolving forever around our Lord, like the planets around the sun. Our Creator looks after us all our lives, so we must obey and be constantly aware of Him; we must avoid things He has banned and do good works that please Him and remember Him "when standing, sitting and lying down, and reflect on the creation of the heavens and the earth." (*Surah Al Imran*, 3:190-191).

Sa'y, or walking briskly between the Safa and Marwa Hills, recalls the great struggle of Ibrahim's wife, Hagar, and her total trust in Allah throughout. Doing as Hagar did some 4000 years ago shows believers how they must "run for God" if necessary.

Talbiya, or the often repeated *labayak* prayer, is a believer's response to God's call. This is a foretaste of the Day of Judgment, when "the trumpet will be blown and behold, they will rise up from their graves and hasten to their Lord." (*Surah Ya Sin*, 36:51).

Zamzam, the spring which gushed forth by God's will, saving the lives of Hagar and her baby Ismail, shows that trusting believers will be duly rewarded by Allah, perhaps even by a miracle. As this water quenches the thirst of millions of pilgrims year after year, without its flow ever stopping, it signals God's immense power and love for His creatures.

Rami, or throwing pebbles at Satan's pillars at Mina, shows how believers must avoid temptation. Whenever their inner "Satan," tempts them to err, they will mentally "throw pebbles" at it to drive it away.

Arafat. Here the Prophet Muhammad ﷺ announced that the really superior person is righteous and God-fearing, taking no pride in colour, creed or position. Assembling at Arafat is, for the pilgrims, like standing before God on Judgement Day.

Muzdalifa, where pilgrims stay overnight, mainly by the roadside. This teaches the same lesson as that of Mina and Arafat, since their lifestyle in small tents has to be very simple. It reminds them of the homeless and the needy, and prompts them to assist others.

The Sacrifice of an animal at Mina (the festival of 'Id) recalls the Prophet Ibrahim's readiness to obey Allah's command to sacrifice his beloved son. Believers, if need be, must likewise be ready to sacrifice their wealth and belongings for God's cause. Of this, the Quran says: "Their flesh and blood do not reach God; it is your piety that reaches Him." (*Surah al-Hajj*, 22:37). It also reminds believers to take care of the needy, especially in their own home towns.

15. The Pilgrims Route

▲ Madinah
277 Miles

◀ Jeddah
45 Miles

● Madinah

● Makkah **Saudi Arabia**

Makkah

● Jabal al-Nur
Site of the first
revelation of the Quran

● Jabal al-Thawr
Site of the cave where
the Prophet took shelter
during his migration

Mina
The Stoning Pillars
Site of the Prophet Ibrahim's
sacrifice.

Muzdalifah
The pilgrims pray here and stay
overnight. They also collect
small stones for throwing at the
stoning pillars in Mina.

Arafat
Site of the Prophet
Muhammad's Farewell
Sermon. Here the pilgrims
participate in the main Hajj
rite, known as the
Standing of Arafat.

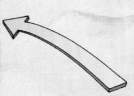

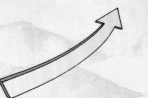

16. Hajj at a Glance

A few days before Hajj:

Put on the pilgrim's dress (*ihram*) at one of the appointed places called *miqats*. (If travelling by air, one may wear *ihram* before boarding the plane.)

Enter the Sacred Mosque of Makkah and perform seven rounds (*tawaf*) of the Kabah, then walk briskly seven times between the Safa and Marwa hills. Trim hair and remove *ihram*.

FIRST DAY:
8th Dhul Hijjah.

Put on *ihram* again, and declare one's intention of performing Hajj. Perform *tawaf* of the Kabah and *sa'y*, if not performed earlier, and leave for Mina early in the morning, reciting *talbiya*. Stay overnight in Mina. This day is known as *Yawm al-Tarwiyah*, or the Day of Reflection.

SECOND DAY:
9th Dhul Hijjah.

Go to Arafat and say the *zuhr* and *asr* prayers together, combined and shortened.
Stand here with devotion, till sunset, praying and asking Allah's forgiveness. This act is known as *wuquf* or standing. This day is known, therefore, as *Yawm al-Wuquf*, or The Day of Standing. In the evening move towards Muzdalifah and say the *maghrib* and *isha* prayers together. Rest there at night, and collect small pebbles for the stoning in Mina.

THIRD DAY:
10th Dhul Hijjah.

Go to Mina and throw small stones there at one of the Jamarat. Offer up a sacrifice and have the hair of the head clipped, trimmed or shaved.
Go to Makkah and perform *tawaf*. (Also go back and forth between Safa and Marwa, if *sa'y* has not been performed on 8th Dhul Hijjah), then return to Mina. This day is called *Yawm al-Nahr*, or the Day of Sacrifice.

FOURTH DAY:
11th Dhul Hijjah

Stay in Mina and throw pebbles at the Jamarat. This day and the next two days are called *Ayyam al-Tashriq*, which literally means, "the days of drying meat."

FIFTH DAY:
12th Dhul Hijjah

Stay in Mina and throw pebbles at the Jamarat. Return the same day to Makkah and perform *tawaf*, then drink the water of the Zamzam. This ends the Hajj.

Note: Those unable to leave Mina for Makkah on 12th Dhul Hijjah should stay at Mina for one more night. The next day, on 13th Dhul Hijjah, after pelting the stoning pillars with stones, they should leave for Makkah in the afternoon.

17. Glossary of Hajj

Afaqi. Pilgrim who comes from outside the appointed *miqats*.

Asr. The afternoon prayer.

Ayyam al-Tashriq. Lit. "the days of drying meat." The 11th, 12th and 13th Dhul Hijjah, during which pilgrims stay in Mina and perform the rites of stoning.

Dum. Making amends for one's shortcomings. See KAFFARAH.

Dhul Hijjah. The twelfth month of the Islamic Calendar during which Hajj is performed.

Fajr. The early morning prayer.

Fard. Duty for every Muslim.

Hady. Animal for sacrifice.

Hajj. Lit. "to set out for a place." Pilgrimage to Makkah, which is one of the five pillars of Islam. It is compulsory for every Muslim, male and female, if he or she possesses enough wealth to undertake the journey and has good health.

Hajj Ifrad. Lit. "isolated pilgrimage." Hajj without *umrah*. A pilgrim who performs it is known as *mufrid*.

Hajj Qiran. Lit. "accompanied pilgrimage." To perform *umrah* and Hajj, one after another, with the same *ihram*. One who does so is called *qarin*.

Hajj Tamattu. Lit. "interrupted pilgrimage." Pilgrimage in which a pilgrim performs *umrah* some time before Hajj and removes *ihram*. When Hajj days approach, the pilgrim puts on *ihram* again for Hajj. One who does so is called *mutamatti*.

Halq, see TAHLIQ.

Id al-Adha. The feast of the sacrifice. The third day of the Hajj—10th Dhul Hijjah, which is celebrated throughout the Muslim world as a great festival.

Ifadah. Lit. "overflowing." The pilgrim's movement from Arafat to Muzdalifah is called *ifadah* or *nafrah* meaning "rush."

Ihram. Lit. "prohibiting." Pilgrim's robe consisting of two seamless white sheets or towels. One of the pieces is wrapped around the midriff to cover the body from just above the navel down to the ankles. The other is draped around the shoulders to cover the upper body. (Women wear scarves covering their heads, along with their usual clothes.) Wearing this is a sign of readiness to enter the sacred land of Makkah in the chastened state of mind appropriate to Hajj. The pilgrim says two *rakat* prayers intended for Hajj or *umrah* at the time of putting on *ihram*.

Isha. The night prayer.

Istilam. Kissing, touching the Black Stone or simply facing towards it at the beginning of each round of *tawaf*.

Kaffarah. Lit. "to hide." Atonement. To offer a sacrifice, etc., for failing to perform certain rites in Hajj. This is also called *dum*.

Khutbah. Sermon given by the *imam* before certain prayers.

Maghrib. The evening prayer.

Mahram. Lit. "unlawful." A close relative whom a woman cannot marry, such as her father, brother, son, etc. A woman going to Hajj should be accompanied by her husband or a *mahram*.

Miqat. Lit. "a stated time or place." Places outside Makkah where the pilgrim puts on *ihram*, before entering Makkah for Hajj or *umrah*.

Muallim or Mutawwif. A guide who assists pilgrims in performing Hajj rites.

Mufrid, see HAJJ IFRAD.

Mutamatti, see HAJJ TAMATTU.

Nafrah, see IFADAH.

Nahr. Animal sacrifice which is made in Mina after the casting of pebbles is completed.

Qarin, see HAJJ QIRAN.

Qibla. The direction of prayer towards the Kabah.

Rafth. Indulging in absurd talk, which is forbidden during Hajj.

Ramal. Proceeding round the Kabah at a jogging pace in the first three rounds of *tawaf*. (Ladies are not required to practice *ramal*).

Ramy. One of the Hajj rites of casting small pebbles at the stone pillars called the Jamarat in Mina.

Rida. The upper cloth of *ihram*.

Sa'y. Lit. "running." One of the Hajj rites of going to and fro between Safa and Marwa seven times.

Salah (pl. *salat*). Five obligatory prayers, performed daily.

Shaut. One circle around the Kabah, or one journey from Safa to Marwa.

Niyyah. Intention. Like all other acts of worship, Hajj and *umrah* require a formal declaration of intention before they are undertaken.

Tahlil. Recitation of *Shahadah*: *La ilaha illal Lah, Muhammadur-rasul Allah.* There is no deity save Allah, Muhammad is the messenger of Allah.

Tahliq or halq. Clipping or shaving the hair of the head after the sacrifice.

Talbiyah. Lit. "to pronounce *labbayk*." The invocation the pilgrim often repeats after wearing *ihram* till the throwing of the pebbles at

the Jamarat. (See RAMY)
The invocation is as follows:

لَبَّيْكَ، اَللّٰهُمَّ لَبَّيْكَ لَبَّيْكَ لَاشَرِيكَ لَكَ لَبَّيْكَ اِنَّ الْحَمْدَ وَالنِّعْمَةَ لَكَ وَالْمُلْكَ لَاشَرِيْكَ لَكَ ٥

Labbayk Allahuma labbayk.
Labbayk la sharika laka labbayk.
Inn al-hamda wan ni'mata laka,
wal mulk, la sharika lak.

Here I am, O Allah! Here I am!
Here I am.
You have no partner, here I am.
Surely Yours is all praise, all goodness and all sovereignty, and You have no partner.

Taqsir. Trimming of the hair after the sacrifice.

Tawaf. A rite of Hajj which is performed by going around the Kabah seven times in an anti-clockwise direction, having the Kabah on the left hand side.

Tawaf al-Ifadah or Tawaf al-Ziyarah. This *tawaf* is performed on 10th Dhul Hijjah.

Tawaf al-Nafl. A *tawaf* which may be performed at any time.

Tawaf al-Qudum. The rite of going around the Kabah on arrival.

Tawaf al-Umrah. A *tawaf* performed during *umrah*.

Tawaf al-Wada. The *tawaf* of farewell, i.e., upon leaving

Makkah. This is not obligatory, but recommended.

Umrah. The lesser pilgrimage, which consists only of the *tawaf* of the Kabah and the *sa'y* of Safa and Marwa. It can be performed at any time during the day or night, all the year round.

Wadu. The washing of hands, face and feet before prayers.

Wuquf. Lit. "standing." Staying in the Arafat valley and especially praying there in the standing position on the second day of Hajj, 9th Dhul Hijjah.

Yawm Arafah. The Day of Arafat. The second day of Hajj, 9th Dhul Hijjah, is also known by this name.

Yawm al-Nahr. The day of sacrifice. The third day of Hajj, 10th Dhul Hijjah, when pilgrims offer a sacrifice at Mina.

Yawm al-Tarwiyah. Lit. "the day of reflection." The first day of Hajj, 8th Dhul Hijjah, when pilgrims move towards Mina.

Yawm al-Wuquf. The day of standing. The second day of Hajj, 9th Dhul Hijjah, when pilgrims stand in Arafat for prayers.

Zuhr. The midday prayer.

---

18. Places of Hajj and Other Historical Sites

Al-Ahzab Mosque. The mosque in Madinah, which is built on the site of the defensive trench dug at the instance of the Prophet Muhammad ﷺ to avoid a confrontation with his enemies.

Arafat. Plain about 12 miles/19 kilometers east of Makkah. It is a major focal point for Hajj. On 9th Dhul Hijjah all pilgrims must present themselves here for the main rite called *wuquf* or "the standing." The Prophet Muhammad ﷺ delivered his last sermon here.

Badr. The town 12 kilometers to the south of Madinah where, during the time of the Prophet Muhammad ﷺ, a small party of Muslims defeated a strong army of Makkan pagans, who had organized an attack on the Muslims.

Bakkah or Becca. Makkah is mentioned in the Quran by this name.

Al-Baqi. The cemetery of Madinah near the Prophet's Mosque, which contains the graves of many notable figures such as the third Caliph Uthman and the Prophet's wife, 'Aishah.

Al-Bayt al-Atiq. The Ancient House. One of the names of the Kabah in the Quran.

Al-Bayt al-Haram. The Sacred House. One of the names of the Kabah in the Quran.

Al-Bayt al-Muharram. The Sacred House. One of the names of the Kabah in the Quran.

The Birthplace of the Prophet. Makkah is the birthplace of the Prophet Muhammad ﷺ. Today a library (Maktaba Makkah) stands on the actual site.

The Black Stone, see HAJR ASWAD.

Burqa. Lit. "the veil." The curtain that covers the door of the Kabah.

The Cave of Hira. The cave atop the Mount of Mercy in Makkah where the Prophet Muhammad ﷺ received the very first revelation of the Quran.

The Cave of Thawr. The cave where the Prophet and his closest Companion, Abu Bakr, took shelter for three nights from the enemy on their *hijrah* (migration) to Madinah. The incident is mentioned in the Quran in *Surah al-Tawbah*, 9:40.

Dar al-Arqam. The house of Arqam, a Companion of the Prophet. His house stood at the foot of the hill called Safa near the Kabah, which was the meeting place of early Muslims.

Five Mosques. Complex in Madinah where five historical mosques are situated. These are Masjid Fath, Masjid Abu Bakr Siddiq, Masjid Salman Farsi, Masjid Umar and Masjid Ali.

Hajr Aswad. The Black Stone. The stone fixed on the eastern corner of the Kabah. This is the only original relic of the times of the Prophet Ibrahim.

Haram. Sacred precincts of the city of Makkah and Madinah.

Al-Harmayn al-Sharifayn. The Two Holy Mosques. The Sacred Mosque at Makkah and the Prophet's Mosque at Madinah.

Hatim. Lit. "the broken part." Semi-circular wall near the Kabah. At one point of time this was part of the Kabah.

Hijaz. The region along the western seaboard of Arabia, in which Makkah, Madinah, Jeddah and Ta'if are situated.

Al-Hudaybiyyah. A place nine miles from Makkah on the road from Makkah to Jeddah. Here the Prophet Muhammad ﷺ signed the famous peace treaty which was referred to in the Quran, *Surah al-Fath*, 48:1 as "an obvious victory."

Hunayn. A valley oasis about 14 miles to the east of Makkah, on the road to Ta'if from Makkah. During the Prophet Muhammad's time the tribes of Hunayn organized an attack on the Muslims.

Jabal Qazah. A mountain in Muzdalifah.

Jabal Takbir. A mountain in Mina.

Jabal Rahmah. The Mountain of Mercy. The mountain in Arafat on which the Prophet Muhammad ﷺ preached his famous sermon, known as the Farwell Sermon.

Jamarat (sing. *jamrah*). The three stone pillars in Mina where the pilgrims throw small pebbles, this being a rite of Hajj. These are called *al-Jamrat al-Kubra* the tallest pillar; *al-Jamrat al-Wusta*, the middle pillar; and *al-Jamrat al-Sughra*, the smallest pillar.

Al-Jumua Mosque. The mosque in Madinah, where the Prophet Muhammad ﷺ offered his Friday prayer.

Kabah. The Kabah, whose name is derived from the Arabic word which means a cube, is the shrine originally built by the Prophet Ibrahim in Makkah, towards which Muslims face while praying.

Khayf Mosque. A mosque in Mina.

Kiswa. The covering of the Kabah.

Maqam Ibrahim. The Standing Place of the Prophet Ibrahim, marked by a small golden kiosk in the vicinity of the Kabah. Two *rakat* prayers are offered here by pilgrims, following the Quran, *Surah al-Baqarah*, 2:125.

Masa. The walkway between Safa and Marwa. See SAFA, MARWA

Al-Mashar al-Haram. The Sacred Monument. A place in Muzdalifah where the Prophet stopped during his Hajj. It is mentioned in the Quran, *Surah al-Baqarah*, 2:198.

Al-Masjid al-Haram, see THE SACRED MOSQUE.

Al-Masjid an-Nabawi. Mosque of the Prophet. One of the three most sacred mosques (the other two are the Sacred Mosque in Makkah and the al-Aqsa mosque in Jerusalem). The Prophet Muhammad after migration to Madinah built this mosque, which became a centre of his activities. The Prophet had his own house within the mosque too. The graves of the Prophet and some of his closest Companions are situated here.

Mataf. Open area around the Kabah where pilgrims perform *tawaf*. See TAWAF.

Maylayn Akhdarayn. The area marked with green pillars where pilgrims move at a jogging pace while performing *sa'y*.

Makkah. *Makkah al-Mukarramah* or Makkah the Blessed, is the city which was first inhabited by the family of the Prophet Ibrahim, who built the Kabah. The Prophet Muhammad ﷺ was born here and today it is the centre of Hajj and the focal point for Muslims all around the world, who turn towards it five times a day in prayer.

Madinah. Formerly known as Yathrib, this city was re-named *Madinat al-Nabi* (the City of the Prophet) or *al-Madinah al-Munawwarah* (The Radiant City) or simply *Madinah* (Madinah), after the migration of the Prophet Muhammad ﷺ here.

Mina. A small town about 3 miles/5 kilometers away from Makkah where, during Hajj, the pilgrims stay in small tents. The rites of throwing pebbles at stone pillars called Jamarat and the sacrifice of animals are carried out here.

Miqat (pl. *mawaqit*). Lit. "appointed place." Certain points where approaching pilgrims for Hajj and *umrah* assume *ihram*. One may imagine these points joined up by a line beyond which pilgrims may not go on to Makkah without wearing *ihram*. Some of the *miqats* are Qarn al-Manazil, 31 miles to the east of Makkah; Yalamlam, 37 miles to the southeast of Makkah; Dhat Irq about 50 miles northeast of the city; Juhfah, 110 miles northwest of the city; and Dhat Hulayfah, about 155 miles north of Makkah. (Pilgrims arriving at Jeddah by air usually put on *ihram* before boarding the plane).

Mizab al-Rahmah. The Spout of Mercy. A golden water-spout jutting out from the north-west of the Kabah through which rain water falls.

Mountain of Light. Jabal al-Nur. The mountain in Makkah on top of which the Cave of Thawr is situated.

The Mosque of the Jinn. The mosque in Makkah where a group of jinn came to the Prophet Muhammad ﷺ and listened to him recite a portion of the Quran. The incident is mentioned in *surah al-Jinn* of the Quran.

Muhssar, see WADI MUHSSAR

Al-Multazam. Lit. "the place to hold on." The wall of the Kabah between its door and the Black Stone. The area is especially sacred, as pilgrims gather here for *du'a*—personal prayer.

Al-Mu'lla. The cemetery of Makkah situated near the Mosque of the Jinn. It contains the graves of the Prophet's wife, Khadijah, his uncle, Abu Talib, his grandfather, Abd al-Muttalib, and many other notable figures.

Muzdalifah. A place 3.5 miles/8 kilometers away from Makkah. Pilgrims on the way from Arafat to Mina stay here overnight and collect small pebbles to throw at the Jamarat in Mina.

Namirah Mosque. The mosque at Arafat where pilgrims recite the combined prayers of *zuhr* and *'asr* on 9th Dhul Hijjah.

Qiblatayn Mosque. The Mosque of Two Qiblas. The Mosque in Madinah where, while praying, the Prophet Muhammad ﷺ was ordered by Allah to change the *qibla* (prayer direction) from Jerusalem to Makkah.

Quba Mosque. The first mosque in Islam built by the Prophet Muhammad ﷺ, after his emigration from Makkah, in a village called Quba just outside Madinah. It later came to be known as the Masjid al-Taqwa (the Mosque of Reverence.)

Rukn Aswad. The Black Stone corner. The eastern corner of the Kabah on which the Black Stone is fixed.

Rukn Iraqi. The Iraqi Corner. The northern corner of the Kabah which faces towards Iraq.

Rukn Shami. The Syrian corner. The western corner of the Kabah which faces towards Syria.

Rukn Yamani. The Yemen corner. The southern corner of the Kabah which faces towards Yemen.

The Sacred Mosque or al-Masjid al-Haram. The gigantic mosque in Makkah, in the centre of which the Kabah stands. The mosque also encloses Safa and Marwa and the Zamzam area.

Safa and Marwa. Two small hills in Makkah near the Kabah (now enclosed within the Sacred Mosque) between which pilgrims go back and forth seven times to re-enact Hagar's search for water for her baby, Ismail ﷺ.

Shadharwan. The marble base, about one foot high, on which the Kabah stands.

Uhud. A mountain outside Madinah about which the Prophet once said, "We love it, and it loves us."

Wadi Muhssar. Also known as Wadi Nar. A place near Mina where, in the year when the Prophet Muhammad ﷺ was born, the Army of the Elephant was punished by Divine intervention. *Surah* 105 of the Quran describes the event.

Well of Uthman. A well traditionally associated with Uthman ibn Affan, one of the Prophet's closest Companions. It is situated in the middle of a date palm orchard, to the north of Madinah.

Zamzam. A well near the Kabah inside the Sacred Mosque, from which pilgrims ritually drink. The Zamzam spring appeared when Hagar and her baby, Ismail, were extremely thirsty in the desert.

19. Prayers from the Quran and the Hadith

"When My servants question you about Me, tell them that I am near. I answer the prayer of every supplicant who calls to Me; therefore let them respond to Me, and believe in Me, that they may be rightly guided." (Surah al-Baqarh 2: 186)

بِسْمِ اللَّهِ الرَّحْمَنِ الرَّحِيمِ ٠
الْحَمْدُ لِلَّهِ رَبِّ الْعَالَمِينَ ٠
الرَّحْمَنِ الرَّحِيمِ ٠ مَالِكِ يَوْمِ الدِّينِ ٠ إِيَّاكَ نَعْبُدُ وَإِيَّاكَ
نَسْتَعِينُ ٠ اهْدِنَا الصِّرَاطَ الْمُسْتَقِيمَ ٠ صِرَاطَ الَّذِينَ أَنْعَمْتَ
عَلَيْهِمْ غَيْرِ الْمَغْضُوبِ عَلَيْهِمْ وَلَا الضَّالِّينَ ٠

Praise to Allah, Lord of the Universe, the Beneficent, the Merciful, Master of the Day of Judgement. You alone we worship, and to You alone we turn for help. Guide us to the straight path. The path of those who have found Your favour, not of those who have incurred Your wrath, nor of those who have gone astray. (1:1-7)

رَبَّنَا آمَنَّا بِمَا أَنْزَلْتَ وَاتَّبَعْنَا الرَّسُولَ فَاكْتُبْنَا مَعَ
الشَّاهِدِينَ ٠

Our Lord! We believe in what You have revealed, and we follow the Messenger; so write us down among those who bear witness. (3:53)

رَبَّنَا لَا تُزِغْ قُلُوبَنَا بَعْدَ إِذْ هَدَيْتَنَا وَهَبْ لَنَا مِن لَّدُنكَ رَحْمَةً
إِنَّكَ أَنتَ الْوَهَّابُ ٠ رَبَّنَا إِنَّكَ جَامِعُ النَّاسِ
لِيَوْمٍ لَّا رَيْبَ فِيهِ إِنَّ اللَّهَ لَا يُخْلِفُ الْمِيعَادَ ٠

Our Lord, do not cause our hearts to go astray after You have guided us. Grant us Your own mercy; You are the generous Giver. Lord, You will surely gather all humanity before You upon a day that will indubitably come. Allah will not break His promise. (3:8-9)

قُلِ اللَّهُمَّ مَالِكَ الْمُلْكِ تُؤْتِي الْمُلْكَ مَن تَشَاءُ وَتَنزِعُ
الْمُلْكَ مِمَّن تَشَاءُ وَتُعِزُّ مَن تَشَاءُ وَتُذِلُّ مَن تَشَاءُ بِيَدِكَ
الْخَيْرُ إِنَّكَ عَلَى كُلِّ شَيْءٍ قَدِيرٌ ٠ تُولِجُ اللَّيْلَ فِي النَّهَارِ
وَتُولِجُ النَّهَارَ فِي اللَّيْلِ وَتُخْرِجُ الْحَيَّ مِنَ الْمَيِّتِ
وَتُخْرِجُ الْمَيِّتَ مِنَ الْحَيِّ وَتَرْزُقُ مَن تَشَاءُ بِغَيْرِ حِسَابٍ ٠

Lord, Sovereign of all sovereignty, You bestow power on whom You will and take it away from whom You please; You exalt whoever You will and abase whoever You please. In Your hand lies all that is good; You have power over all things. You cause the night to pass into the day and the day into the night; You bring forth the living from the dead and the dead from the living. You give without measure to whom You will. (3:26-27)

وَقُل رَّبِّ زِدْنِي عِلْمًا ٠

Lord, increase my knowledge. (20:114)

رَبَّنَا لَا تُؤَاخِذْنَا إِن نَّسِينَا أَوْ أَخْطَأْنَا رَبَّنَا وَلَا تَحْمِلْ
عَلَيْنَا إِصْرًا كَمَا حَمَلْتَهُ عَلَى الَّذِينَ مِن قَبْلِنَا رَبَّنَا وَلَا
تُحَمِّلْنَا مَا لَا طَاقَةَ لَنَا بِهِ وَاعْفُ عَنَّا وَاغْفِرْ لَنَا وَارْحَمْنَا
أَنتَ مَوْلَانَا فَانصُرْنَا عَلَى الْقَوْمِ الْكَافِرِينَ ٠

Our Lord, take us not to task if we forget, or lapse into error. Our Lord, charge us not with the burden You laid upon those before us. Our Lord, do not burden us beyond what we have the strength to bear. And pardon us, and forgive us our sins, and have mercy on us, You alone are our Protector. And help us against people who deny the truth. (2:286)

إِنَّ فِي خَلْقِ السَّمَاوَاتِ وَالْأَرْضِ وَاخْتِلَافِ اللَّيْلِ
وَالنَّهَارِ لَآيَاتٍ لِّأُولِي الْأَلْبَابِ ٠ الَّذِينَ يَذْكُرُونَ اللَّهَ
قِيَامًا وَقُعُودًا وَعَلَى جُنُوبِهِمْ وَيَتَفَكَّرُونَ فِي خَلْقِ
السَّمَاوَاتِ وَالْأَرْضِ رَبَّنَا مَا خَلَقْتَ هَذَا بَاطِلًا سُبْحَانَكَ
فَقِنَا عَذَابَ النَّارِ ٠ رَبَّنَا إِنَّكَ مَن تُدْخِلِ النَّارَ فَقَدْ
أَخْزَيْتَهُ وَمَا لِلظَّالِمِينَ مِنْ أَنصَارٍ ٠ رَبَّنَا إِنَّنَا
سَمِعْنَا مُنَادِيًا يُنَادِي لِلْإِيمَانِ أَنْ آمِنُوا بِرَبِّكُمْ فَآمَنَّا
رَبَّنَا فَاغْفِرْ لَنَا ذُنُوبَنَا وَكَفِّرْ عَنَّا سَيِّئَاتِنَا وَتَوَفَّنَا
مَعَ الْأَبْرَارِ ٠ رَبَّنَا وَآتِنَا مَا وَعَدتَّنَا عَلَى رُسُلِكَ وَلَا
تُخْزِنَا يَوْمَ الْقِيَامَةِ إِنَّكَ لَا تُخْلِفُ الْمِيعَادَ ٠

Surely, in the creation of the heavens and earth, and in the alternation of night and day there are signs for people of sense, (those) who remember Allah, standing and sitting and lying down to sleep, and reflect upon the creation of the heavens and the earth: 'Our Lord You have not created this (universe) in vain. Glory be to You! Save us from the suffering of the Fire. Our Lord, those whom You will cast into the Fire, You will put to eternal shame; and the evildoers shall have no helpers. Our Lord, we have heard the call of one calling us to the true faith, saying, "Believe in the Lord!" And we believed. Our Lord, forgive us our sins and remove from us our bad deeds, and take our souls to Yourself with the righteous. Our Lord, grant us what You have promised us through Your Messengers, and save us from disgrace on the Day of Resurrection; You will never break Your promise!' (3:190-194)

قُلْ إِنَّ صَلَاتِي وَنُسُكِي وَمَحْيَايَ وَمَمَاتِي لِلَّهِ رَبِّ الْعَالَمِينَ ٠

Say 'My prayer, my worship, my living, my dying are for Allah alone, the lord of all Being.' (6:162)

قَالَا رَبَّنَا ظَلَمْنَا أَنفُسَنَا وَإِن لَّمْ تَغْفِرْ لَنَا وَتَرْحَمْنَا لَنَكُونَنَّ مِنَ
الْخَاسِرِينَ ٠

Lord, we have wronged our souls. Pardon us and have mercy on us, or we shall surely be among the lost. (7:23)

رَبَّنَآ أَفۡرِغۡ عَلَيۡنَا صَبۡرًا وَتَوَفَّنَا مُسۡلِمِينَ ○

Lord, give us patience and let us die in submission. (7:126)

أَنتَ وَلِيُّنَا فَٱغۡفِرۡ لَنَا وَٱرۡحَمۡنَا وَأَنتَ خَيۡرُ ٱلۡغَٰفِرِينَ ○ وَٱكۡتُبۡ لَنَا فِي هَٰذِهِ ٱلدُّنۡيَا حَسَنَةً وَفِي ٱلۡأٓخِرَةِ إِنَّا هُدۡنَآ إِلَيۡكَ ○

Lord, You alone are our Guardian. Forgive us and have mercy on us: You are the noblest of those who forgive. Ordain for us what is good, both in this life and in the Hereafter. To You alone we turn. (7:155-156)

رَبَّنَآ ءَاتِنَا مِن لَّدُنكَ رَحۡمَةً وَهَيِّئۡ لَنَا مِنۡ أَمۡرِنَا رَشَدًا ○

Our Lord! Send upon us Your mercy, and show us the solution to our problem in the right way. (18:10)

قَالَ رَبِّ ٱشۡرَحۡ لِي صَدۡرِي ○ وَيَسِّرۡ لِيٓ أَمۡرِي ○ وَٱحۡلُلۡ عُقۡدَةً مِّن لِّسَانِي ○ يَفۡقَهُوا۟ قَوۡلِي ○ وَٱجۡعَل لِّي وَزِيرًا مِّنۡ أَهۡلِي ○ هَٰرُونَ أَخِي ○ ٱشۡدُدۡ بِهِۦٓ أَزۡرِي ○ وَأَشۡرِكۡهُ فِيٓ أَمۡرِي ○ كَيۡ نُسَبِّحَكَ كَثِيرًا ○ وَنَذۡكُرَكَ كَثِيرًا ○ إِنَّكَ كُنتَ بِنَا بَصِيرًا ○

Lord, put courage into my heart, and ease my task for me. Free the knot of my tongue, that they may understand my message. Appoint for me among my kinsmen one who will help me bear my burden, Harun, my brother; by him add to my strength, and let him share with me in my tasks, so that we may give glory to You, and remember You without ceasing. Surely You are watching over us. (20:25-35)

رَبِّ أَوۡزِعۡنِيٓ أَنۡ أَشۡكُرَ نِعۡمَتَكَ ٱلَّتِيٓ أَنۡعَمۡتَ عَلَيَّ وَعَلَىٰ وَٰلِدَيَّ وَأَنۡ أَعۡمَلَ صَٰلِحًا تَرۡضَىٰهُ وَأَدۡخِلۡنِي بِرَحۡمَتِكَ فِي عِبَادِكَ ٱلصَّٰلِحِينَ ○

Inspire me, Lord, that I may forever be grateful for the blessings You have bestowed on me and on my parents, and that I may do good works that will please You and include me through Your mercy amongst Your righteous servants. (27:19)

وَقُل رَّبِّ أَدۡخِلۡنِي مُدۡخَلَ صِدۡقٍ وَأَخۡرِجۡنِي مُخۡرَجَ صِدۡقٍ وَٱجۡعَل لِّي مِن لَّدُنكَ سُلۡطَٰنًا نَّصِيرًا ○

Lord, grant me a goodly entrance and a goodly exit, and sustain me with Your power. (17:80)

رَّبِّ أَعُوذُ بِكَ مِنۡ هَمَزَٰتِ ٱلشَّيَٰطِينِ ○ وَأَعُوذُ بِكَ رَبِّ أَن يَحۡضُرُونِ ○

Lord, I seek refuge in You from the promptings of all evil impulses. Lord, I seek refuge with You from their presence. (23:98-99)

رَبَّنَآ ءَامَنَّا فَٱغۡفِرۡ لَنَا وَٱرۡحَمۡنَا وَأَنتَ خَيۡرُ ٱلرَّٰحِمِينَ ○

Our lord, we believe; therefore forgive us, and have mercy on us, for You are the best of the merciful. (23:109)

رَبَّنَا هَبۡ لَنَا مِنۡ أَزۡوَٰجِنَا وَذُرِّيَّٰتِنَا قُرَّةَ أَعۡيُنٍ وَٱجۡعَلۡنَا لِلۡمُتَّقِينَ إِمَامًا ○

Lord, give us joy in our spouses and children and make us foremost among those who are conscious of You. (25:74)

رَبِّ إِنِّي لِمَآ أَنزَلۡتَ إِلَيَّ مِنۡ خَيۡرٍ فَقِيرٌ ○

Lord, I stand in dire need of any good which You may bestow upon me! (28:24)

أَنِّي مَغۡلُوبٌ فَٱنتَصِرۡ ○

Help me, Lord, I am overcome! (54:10)

رَبِّ أَوۡزِعۡنِيٓ أَنۡ أَشۡكُرَ نِعۡمَتَكَ ٱلَّتِيٓ أَنۡعَمۡتَ عَلَيَّ وَعَلَىٰ وَٰلِدَيَّ وَأَنۡ أَعۡمَلَ صَٰلِحًا تَرۡضَىٰهُ وَأَصۡلِحۡ لِي فِي ذُرِّيَّتِيٓ إِنِّي تُبۡتُ إِلَيۡكَ وَإِنِّي مِنَ ٱلۡمُسۡلِمِينَ ○

Inspire me, my Lord that I may be thankful for Your blessing bestowed on me and my parents, and that I may do good works that will please You. Grant me good descendants. To You I turn and to You I surrender myself. (46:15)

قَالَ رَبِّ إِنِّي ظَلَمۡتُ نَفۡسِي فَٱغۡفِرۡ لِي ○

My Lord, Forgive me! for I have sinned against my soul. (28:16)

سُبۡحَٰنَ ٱلَّذِي سَخَّرَ لَنَا هَٰذَا وَمَا كُنَّا لَهُۥ مُقۡرِنِينَ ○ وَإِنَّآ إِلَىٰ رَبِّنَا لَمُنقَلِبُونَ ○

Glory to be to Him, who has subjected these to us. We ourselves were not able to subdue them. To our Lord we shall all return. (43:13-14)

رَبَّنَا ٱغۡفِرۡ لَنَا وَلِإِخۡوَٰنِنَا ٱلَّذِينَ سَبَقُونَا بِٱلۡإِيمَٰنِ وَلَا تَجۡعَلۡ فِي قُلُوبِنَا غِلًّا لِّلَّذِينَ ءَامَنُوا۟ رَبَّنَآ إِنَّكَ رَءُوفٌ رَّحِيمٌ ○

Forgive us Lord, and forgive our brothers who embraced the Faith before us. Do not put in our hearts any malice towards the faithful. Lord, You are Compassionate and Merciful. (59:10)

رَبَّنَا ٱغۡفِرۡ لَنَا ذُنُوبَنَا وَإِسۡرَافَنَا فِيٓ أَمۡرِنَا وَثَبِّتۡ أَقۡدَامَنَا وَٱنصُرۡنَا عَلَى ٱلۡقَوۡمِ ٱلۡكَٰفِرِينَ ○

Our Lord! Forgive us our sins and the lack of moderation in our doings. Make our steps firm, and help us against those who deny the faith. (3:147)

ٱللَّهُمَّ إِنِّي أَسۡأَلُكَ ٱلۡهُدَىٰ، وَٱلتُّقَىٰ، وَٱلۡعَفَافَ وَٱلۡغِنَىٰ ○

O Allah, I ask You for guidance, piety, uprightness and prosperity. (Related by Muslim.)

ٱللَّهُمَّ أَصۡلِحۡ لِي دِينِي ٱلَّذِي هُوَ عِصۡمَةُ أَمۡرِي، وَأَصۡلِحۡ لِي دُنۡيَايَ ٱلَّتِي فِيهَا مَعَاشِي، وَأَصۡلِحۡ لِي آخِرَتِي ٱلَّتِي فِيهَا مَعَادِي، وَٱجۡعَلِ ٱلۡحَيَاةَ زِيَادَةً لِي فِي كُلِّ خَيۡرٍ، وَٱجۡعَلِ ٱلۡمَوۡتَ رَاحَةً لِي مِنۡ كُلِّ شَرٍّ ○

O Allah, put my religion in order for me, which is the basis of my affairs. Put in order for me my worldly affairs which are the source of my livelihood. Put in order for me my life in the Hereafter, which is my ultimate destination. Increase all that is good in my life and make death a respite for me from every evil. (Related by Muslim.)

اللَّهُمَّ إِنِّى أَعُوذُبِكَ مِنَ الْعَجْزِ، وَالْكَسَلِ، وَالْجُبْنِ، وَالْبُخْلِ، وَالْهَرَمِ وَعَذَابِ الْقَبْرِ، اللَّهُمَّ آتِ نَفْسِى تَقْوَاهَا، وَزَكِّهَا، وَأَنْتَ خَيْرُ مَنْ زَكَّاهَا. أَنْتَ وَلِيُّهَا وَمَوْلَاهَا. اللَّهُمَّ إِنِّى أَعُوذُبِكَ مِنْ عِلْمٍ لَا يَنْفَعُ، وَمِنْ قَلْبٍ لَا يَخْشَعُ، وَمِنْ نَفْسٍ لَا تَشْبَعُ، وَمِنْ دَعْوَةٍ لَا يُسْتَجَابُ لَهَا ○

O Allah, I seek refuge in You from weakness, laziness, cowardliness, meanness, senility and the punishment of the grave. O Allah, give my soul sufficient piety to fear You, and purify it, as You are the best one who can purify it. You are its Patron and Master. O Allah, I seek refuge in You from knowledge which is of no benefit, a heart which has no fear, an appetite which is insatiable and a supplication which is not answered. (Related by Muslim.)

اَللَّهُمَّ اهْدِنِى وَسَدِّدْنِى، اللَّهُمَّ إِنِّى أَسْأَلُكَ الْهُدَى وَالسَّدَادَ ○

O Allah, guide me and keep me to what is right. O Allah, I ask You for guidance and to keep me on the right path. (Related by Muslim.)

اللَّهُمَّ إِنِّى أَعُوذُ بِكَ مِنْ زَوَالِ نِعْمَتِكَ، وَتَحَوُّلِ عَافِيَتِكَ، وَفُجَاءَةِ نِقْمَتِكَ، وَجَمِيعِ سَخَطِكَ ○

O Allah, I seek refuge in You from the absence of Your favours, a change in Your granting me well-being, a sudden vengeance wrought by You and all that displeases You. (Related by Muslim.)

اللَّهُمَّ إِنِّى أَعُوذُبِكَ مِنْ شَرِّ مَا عَمِلْتُ، وَمِنْ شَرِّ مَا لَمْ أَعْمَلْ ○

O Allah, I seek refuge in You from the evil which I have done and the evil which I have not done. (Related by Muslim.)

اللَّهُمَّ أَكْثِرْ مَالِى، وَوَلَدِى، وَبَارِكْ لِى فِيْمَا أَعْطَيْتَنِى [وَأَطِلْ حَيَاتِىْ عَلى طَاعَتِكَ وَأَحْسِنْ عَمَلِىْ] وَاغْفِرْلِىْ ○

O Allah, increase my wealth, my children and bless me in what You have granted me. Make my life longer upon your obedience, make my deeds the best and forgive me. (Related by al-Bukhari and Muslim.)

لَا إِلٰهَ إِلَّا اللهُ الْعَظِيْمُ الْحَلِيْمُ، لَا إِلٰهَ إِلَّا اللهُ رَبُّ الْعَرْشِ الْعَظِيْمِ، لَا إِلٰهَ إِلَّا اللهُ رَبُّ السَّمٰوَاتِ، وَرَبُّ الْأَرْضِ، وَرَبُّ الْعَرْشِ الْكَرِيْمِ ○

There is no deity which has the right to be worshipped except Allah alone, the Mighty, the Wise. There is no deity which has the right to be worshipped except Allah alone, Lord of the Mighty throne. There is no deity which has the right to be worshipped except Allah alone, Lord of the Heavens, the earth and the Noble Throne. (Related by al-Bukhari and Muslim.)

اللَّهُمَّ رَحْمَتَكَ أَرْجُو فَلَا تَكِلْنِى إِلَى نَفْسِى طَرْفَةَ عَيْنٍ، وَأَصْلِحْ لِى شَأْنِى كُلَّهُ، لَا إِلٰهَ إِلَّا أَنْتَ ○

O Allah, I hope for Your mercy, so do not leave me to myself even for an instant. Set all of my affairs in order. There is no deity which has the right to be worshipped except You alone. (Related by Abu Da'ud and Ahmad.)

اللَّهُمَّ إِنِّى أَسْأَلُكَ الْعَافِيَةَ فِى الدُّنْيَا وَالآخِرَةِ ○

Allah, I ask You for well-being in this life and the Hereafter. (Related by al-Tirmidhi.)

اللَّهُمَّ إِنِّى عَبْدُكَ ابْنُ عَبْدِكَ، ابْنُ أَمَتِكَ، نَاصِيَتِى بِيَدِكَ، مَاضٍ فِىَّ حُكْمُكَ، عَدْلٌ فِىَّ قَضَاؤُكَ. أَسْأَلُكَ بِكُلِّ اسْمٍ هُوَ لَكَ سَمَّيْتَ بِهِ نَفْسَكَ، أَوْ أَنْزَلْتَهُ فِى كِتَابِكَ، أَوْ عَلَّمْتَهُ أَحَداً مِنْ خَلْقِكَ، أَوِ اسْتَأْثَرْتَ بِهِ فِى عِلْمِ الْغَيْبِ عِنْدَكَ، أَنْ تَجْعَلَ الْقُرْآنَ رِبِيْعَ قَلْبِىْ، وَنُوْرَ صَدْرِىْ، وَجَلَاءَ حُزْنِى، وَذَهَابَ هَمِّىْ ○

O Allah, indeed I am Your servant, the son of Your servant and the son of Your female servant. I am under the control of Your Hand. Your Judgement on me shall come to pass and Your Judgement on me is just. I ask of You by all the Names by which You have named Yourself, or revealed in Your book, or taught to any of Your creation, or You have kept hidden in the matters of the unseen with You: Make the Qur'an the spring of my heart and the light of my life. Take away my sorrow and my worries. (Related by Ahmad and al-Haakim.)

اللَّهُمَّ مُصَرِّفَ الْقُلُوبِ صَرِّفْ قُلُوبَنَا عَلى طَاعَتِكَ ○

O Allah, the turner of the hearts, set our hearts upon obedience to You. (Related by Muslim.)

يَا مُقَلِّبَ الْقُلُوبِ ثَبِّتْ قَلْبِى عَلى دِيْنِكَ ○

O Turner of the hearts, make my heart firm upon Your religion. (Related by al-Tirmidhi, Ahmad and al-Haakim.)

يَأَيَّتُهَاالنَّفْسُ الْمُطْمَئِنَّةُ ○ ارْجِعِى إِلَى رَبِّكِ رَاضِيَةً مَرْضِيَّةً ○ فَادْخُلِى فِى عِبَادِى ○ وَأَدْخُلِى جَنَّتِى ○

O soul at peace, return to your Lord, well,pleased, well,pleasing! Join My servants! Enter My Paradise!' (89:27-30)

SELECT BIBLIOGRAPHY

Amin, Mohammed. *Pilgrimage to Makkah*, Nairobi, Camerapix, 1978.

Frika, Abdelaziz and Guellouz Ezzedine. Makkah: *The Muslim Pilgrimage*, London, Paddington Press, 1979.

Glassè, Cyril. *Concise Encyclopaedia of Islam*, London, Stacey International, 1989.

Kadi, Hamza. *Makkah and Madinah Today*, Les Editions, j.a. Paris, 1980.

Khan, Maulana Wahiduddin. *Haqiqat-e-Hajj*, New Delhi, Al-Risala, 1986.

Maqsood, Ruqaiyyah Waris. *Islam*, Oxford, Heinemann Educational, 1996.

Nawwab, Ni'mah Isamil. "Hajj: The Journey of a Lifetime," *Aramco World*, July-August 1992.

Nomachi, Ali Kazuyoshi and Nasr, Seyyed Hossein. *Makkah: The Blessed, Madinah: The Radiant—The Holiest Cities of Islam*, Hong Kong, Odyssey Books, 1997.

Stewart, Desmond and Amin, Mohamed. *Makkah*, New York, Newsweek, 1980.

The Two Holy Mosques, London, Saudi Arabia Information Centre, 1993.